CHOICES AND CHALLENGES

Stewardship Strategies for Youth

DAN R. DICK

DISCIPLESHIP RESOURCES

MATERIALS FOR GROWTH IN CHRISTIAN FAITH & LIFE

—— NASHVILLE, TENNESSEE ——

❖ **TO PLACE AN ORDER** OR TO INQUIRE ABOUT RESOURCES AND CUSTOMER ACCOUNTS, CONTACT:

DISCIPLESHIP RESOURCES DISTRIBUTION CENTER
P.O. BOX 6996
ALPHARETTA, GEORGIA 30239-6996

TEL: (800) 685-4370

FAX: (404) 442-5114

❖ ❖ ❖

❖ **FOR EDITORIAL INQUIRIES** AND RIGHTS AND PERMISSIONS REQUESTS, CONTACT:

DISCIPLESHIP RESOURCES EDITORIAL OFFICES
P.O. BOX 840
NASHVILLE, TENNESSEE 37202-0840

TEL: (615) 340-7068

ISBN 0-88177-135-X

Library of Congress Catalog Card No. 94-72155

Cover design by Graphic Matters.

Unless otherwise indicated, all scripture quotations are taken from the New Revised Standard Version of the Holy Bible, © 1989 by the Division of Christian Education of the National Council of Churches of Christ in the United States of America and are used by permission.

DR135

CONTENTS

Foreword   *v*

Introduction   *vii*

1. TIME ON OUR HANDS   1

2. HAVE A HEART   9

3. STUFF!   19

4. CHOOSE LIFE!   31

   CONCLUSION   41

   GROUP HELPS   45

   A WORSHIP OPTION   59

FOREWORD

This material has been designed primarily for use in a youth group setting; however, with a minimum of creative adaptation it can be modified to work as a Sunday school class program, a weekend retreat format, or as the topical guideline for a week-long stewardship camp. It also has merit as an individual study, easily used apart from a group. The material can be led by an adult group leader or, in the case of teenagers and young adults, it can easily be peer-led.

The study is divided into four main topics for exploration, and, ideally, each section will require approximately ninety minutes to two hours to complete. This provides enough material for a six- to eight-week youth fellowship study, or a twelve-week Sunday school class. A suggested format might be:

Gathering and Prayer	*5 minutes*
Introduction to Theme	*10 minutes*
Dilemmas	*20-30 minutes*
Biblical Reflections	*20-30 minutes*
Practical Applications	*20-30 minutes*
Questions and Concluding Comments	*10 minutes*
Closing and Prayer	*5 minutes*

Given the time constraints, not all Dilemmas, Biblical Reflections, and Practical Applications can be used, and it is vital to keep discussion moving along. By incorporating the Helps in the back of the book, the study can easily be expanded for use in a retreat or camp setting.

One of the important elements of this book is that each subject is interconnected, involving a great deal of group building. It is therefore recommended that, before you begin this journey together, you draft a covenant whereby every member commits to attend all sessions. It is vital that the group dynamic not be disturbed. Stewardship begins with commitment, and priority needs to be given to making this promise to one another.

One last suggestion, that both individuals and groups may find helpful, is to keep a notebook or journal during this course of study. Space is limited within the study guide, and many of the questions call for some indepth answers. Notes and reflections on the reading and Bible passages may be helpful during group discussion. A journal will allow you to personalize this study in a meaningful way.

It is my hope that this material can speak to many different people in many different settings, and that it opens the door to a whole new way of looking at our place in the world as stewards of all that God has given us. May your journey through this work be meaningful and inspirational.

Dan Dick
Pentecost 1994

INTRODUCTION

C hoices. We make literally hundreds of them each day—big ones, small ones, insignificant ones, life-changing ones. No two are exactly alike. We make so many choices that we're not even aware we're making them. How do we know when the choices we make are good ones? Is there any way to be sure that what we reject may not better than what we select?

In the study that follows, we will look at the kinds of choices we make, weigh the positives and negatives, listen to what our Bible has to say about these issues, and share insights into how we might make better choices each day. These are central elements of what is known as *stewardship*.

Stewardship is defined in many different ways. For the benefit of this study we will speak of stewardship *as an individual's way of responding to God for the gifts God gives*. Not all of God's gifts are things we can touch and see. Often God gives us gifts that we can't hold onto; therefore, we take them for granted. Time is a gift. Our relationships with family, friends, and neighbors also are gifts. Our possessions come to us through the goodness of God. Even the earth that we walk on, the air that we breathe, and the water we drink and wash with are gifts from God. When we open our eyes to see that "the earth is the Lord's and all that is in it" (Psalm 24:1), we begin to understand God's goodness; and the way we respond to that goodness, the way we use our time, how we treat other people, how we value things, and how we care for the earth become very important. That response is our stewardship.

Our stewardship, then, hinges on two very important concepts: management and appreciation. The Greek word from which we derive the terms *steward* and *stewardship* actually means "manager of the household." The "manager of the household" was usually a servant who displayed a deep commitment to his master and proved he could deal in business and personal relationships with skill and tact. The master placed a great deal of money and power in the hands of the steward.

As Christians, it is important that we come to understand we are God's stewards. We are entrusted with many gifts from God and have a responsibility to take good care of them. What keeps that responsibility from being a burden is the honest appreciation of how very good and wonderful God's gifts are and a gratitude to God for allowing us to benefit from them while they are in our care. As our appreciation and gratitude increase, so does our commitment to manage wisely. As grateful and faithful managers, we become good stewards, and the choices we make and the priorities we set reflect our stewardship.

We often make choices without thinking about whether they are good ones. We don't look too closely at how our choices are made or what their ramifications may be. God, however, is very interested in the decisions we make; so we should strive for choices that are sound. Learning to make good choices, grounded in our faith and values, is a talent that takes practice to perfect; but when we master it, we truly please God and we assume for ourselves the identity of the faithful steward.

This guidebook is designed to help individuals reflect on their identity as stewards and share their insights in a group setting. There are four main sections for reflection and discussion: (1) STEWARDSHIP OF TIME, (2) STEWARDSHIP OF RELATIONSHIPS, (3) STEWARDSHIP OF MONEY AND POSSESSIONS, and (4) STEWARDSHIP OF OUR GLOBAL COMMUNITY. These themes overlap in many different ways, and the insights gained from them apply equally well to other areas of stewardship.

Within each chapter, the study is divided into three parts. The first part is entitled, DILEMMAS. DILEMMAS are stories that raise stewardship issues and ask you to think about their implication and meaning. The point of the DILEMMAS is to stimulate thinking and to help you focus on what you believe and feel. The purpose is not to figure out right or wrong answers. Many stewardship issues are not so cut and dried. As individuals, we tend to take different approaches to similar problems. We all manage in different ways. This diversity is what makes the body of Christ so great. Look at the DILEMMAS as a way to see just how big an issue stewardship is, and how important it is to see ourselves as stewards of time, relationships, money, and our world.

The second part of each chapter, BIBLICAL REFLECTIONS, turns to the Bible to see what scripture has to say about each theme. These passages are in no way comprehensive. They merely scratch the surface, but they do give us a feel for how God expects us to respond to the gifts we have been given. Once more, the emphasis is not on right and wrong but on how we respond to God. Questions are provided for personal reflection and group discussion.

The last section of each chapter, PRACTICAL APPLICATIONS, contains some exercises to help us take concrete, specific steps toward more faithful stewardship. The PRACTICAL APPLICATIONS build on the themes raised in the DILEMMAS and BIBLICAL REFLECTIONS and show us how to put our ideas into action. They challenge us to make covenants with ourselves, with each other, and with God that will help us grow in our stewardship.

In the back of the book, there are two supplemental sections. The first is a selection of GROUP HELPS for each topic in the study. These helps offer suggestions for activities, further investigation of themes, and ways to illustrate issues raised in each chapter. These helps may prove most useful in youth group and retreat settings. The second supplemental section, A WORSHIP OPTION, is a brief worship celebration that allows the group to celebrate the gifts God gives us and to make a covenant commitment to faithful stewardship.

Consider this study as a journey. In the course of this journey, you will travel to places you have been before and to places you have never been. You will see old things, new things, and, hopefully, old things *in new ways*. God is calling each one of us. God extends to us many wonderful gifts. They are ours for the taking, but we have a choice to make. Will we honor God by taking care of these gifts or dishonor God by taking them for granted? Let us choose wisely. God is watching!

1 | TIME ON OUR HANDS

Don't say you don't have enough time. You have exactly the same number of hours per day that were given to Helen Keller, Louis Pasteur, Leonardo da Vinci, Mother Teresa, Michelangelo, Thomas Jefferson, and Albert Einstein.

H. Jackson Brown, Jr.
Life's Little Instruction Book *

There are only so many hours in each day, but there are so many interesting and exciting things to do. Not only do we have things that we like to do, but other people have ideas about how we should use our time. Parents, teachers, bosses, coaches, band directors, and a hundred other people make demands on our precious time. How can we ever sort out which things are worth our time and which are not?

There is nothing easy about setting priorities concerning our use of time. Businesses run elaborate "time management" seminars, yet no one has ever come up with the one ultimate, sure-fire system that makes everything fit our waking hours. The reason for this is simple: There is no one "right way" to manage time. Sure, some ways are better than others, but every individual will eventually have to decide what is "right" and what works for him or her.

Too often we try to find the "right" way to do something. We search for a one-size-fits-all solution that takes the responsibility off our

---

* *Life's Little Instruction Book* © 1991 by H. Jackson Brown, Jr. and reprinted by permission of Rutledge Hill Press, Nashville, Tennessee.

shoulders to make a choice. It's never that easy. Instead of looking for the right answer, we need to seek the best answer for us individually. Philosopher Mortimer J. Adler speaks often of the "normative perspective." This is the place from which we view all of life—from inside our own heads, hearts, feelings, and experiences. Each person sees the world in a unique way. Therefore, it is highly unlikely that we will ever find one way to manage our lives that works for everyone. The best we can hope for is to find the way that works best for *us*.

There is one fundamental truth about time that is important to keep in mind: Once lost, it can never be recovered. No one knows just how much time she or he has on this planet, and for that reason it's wise to make the most of every day. If we don't pay much attention to where our time goes, it will slip right through our fingers, and we'll be left standing, scratching our heads, wondering where it went. The wise time steward knows where the time goes. Wasted time is kept at a minimum, work gets done in time, and time for enjoyment and other important things in life—such as other people and art and music—is plentiful. Without stewardship we won't be able to manage our time well. We have to make it happen; we have to choose to be in control of our time, or we will lose it.

As you reflect on the questions and issues raised during this study, focus less on finding "right" answers and focus more on gaining insights into what might help you become a good and faithful steward of the Lord Jesus Christ.

Dilemmas

#1 Stacey was really unhappy that the injury made her give up track, but in a way it was the best thing. Her grades were slipping. She hadn't learned half the new music in band. She barely had any money because she hadn't been able to babysit for weeks. And she kept falling asleep in school because she wasn't getting enough sleep. She had even missed church for the last three Sundays because she couldn't drag herself out of bed early enough. Stacey was feeling wiped out most of the time, but she didn't want to give up any of her activities because they were all important to her. She had even decided to try out for the spring musical at school since she couldn't run track, but her mom had hit the roof and told her there was no way she was going to add another activity to her schedule. Her mom had always encouraged her before to be involved. Stacey couldn't believe her mom was turning into such a nag now. Stacey wasn't trying to do any more than many of her friends; she just had a lot that she wanted to do.

1. What are the time issues in this dilemma?

2. What advice or suggestions might you give to Stacey? To her mother?

3. Would it help Stacey if she were given an eighth day each week to "catch up"? Why, or why not?

4. If Stacey is happy trying to do everything, then why should she cut back?

#2 Craig never got his homework done. It wasn't that he didn't try—he just wasn't going to spend his whole life doing homework. He had friends, sports, a girlfriend, and a job where he put in ten hours a week. His parents made him go to bed by 10:00 during the school week, so he couldn't do homework late at night, which was his best time of day. Craig hardly ever had time to watch TV or listen to his music, so he usually turned on the television or put on his Walkman while he studied. His grades weren't great, but they weren't terrible. His parents kept threatening to ground him, but that was no big deal. If he got grounded, he sure wasn't going to use the time to study. If he studied around the clock, it wouldn't make that much difference. He probably still wouldn't get all his home-work done.

1. What are the time issues at work in this scene?

2. How does Craig prioritize his time? How is he a time manager?

3. If stewardship is the way we respond to the gifts we've been given by God, what other stewardship issues besides time are brought out in this story?

4. How does Craig's "time stewardship" reflect what is truly impor-tant to him?

#3 Kim was really mad at Tanya. Every time the two of them made plans, she had to remind Tanya to be on time. Tanya always laughed and told her she would, then she would show up late. It was so rude. Kim never made people wait; she always tried to be on time. It really wasn't any big deal to show up when you were supposed to. Tanya didn't even wear a watch! It was as if she couldn't care less. Tanya had a lot of good qualities, but being on time wasn't one of them. It always made Kim feel as if Tanya didn't value their friend-ship very much if she couldn't even show up on time. After all, if people really cared about others, they would at least make an effort to not keep them waiting all the time.

1. What are the time issues in this story?

2. Why do some people put such importance on "being on time," while other people seem not to care that much?

3. Do we have a responsibility to use our time for others as well as for ourselves?

4. How might you help Kim and Tanya deal with their different ways of managing time?

Biblical Reflections

PRAYER: God of all time—past, present, and future—help us remember that you have given exactly the same number of hours in the day to each one of us, and that these hours are precious and unique. Once lost, they can never be reclaimed. Teach us to be good and faithful stewards of the time that you so graciously grant us. Show us the value of each passing moment, that we might use each one wisely and well. Be proud of our efforts to make the most of each day, and forgive those occasions when we are guilty of wasting time. We pray these things in Jesus' name. Amen.

Listed below are a number of biblical passages that relate to the topic of time. In groups of three or four, look up the passages and read them aloud. Use the questions provided to help explore the guidance the Bible gives us for being stewards of the gift of time.

Ecclesiastes 3:1-8   Ephesians 5:15-16

1. It may seem that these two passages are saying opposite things. What is the main point of each passage? How do the two passages differ? How are they the same?

2. Why is it important to make the most of time in evil days?

3. How can learning to accept the highs and lows of life (as Ecclesiastes suggests) help us become better stewards of the gift of time?

James 4:13-17   Luke 12:13-21

1. What message do you receive from these two passages?

2. What message do you think these scriptures hold for our culture?

3. Why do people tend to think more about their own immediate future instead of trying to see the "big picture" of the long-range future of their community, their country, and their world?

1 Peter 4:7-11

1. This passage makes the stewardship of time, indeed of all gifts, a big deal. There is a real urgency to the way we use our gifts. How might the way we use our time honor God? In what ways might our use of time be considered wrong or sinful?

2. Suppose you were hired by God to write a simple three-line statement explaining how God wants us to use the gift of time. What would that statement be?

3. When a pastor is ordained into The United Methodist Church, she or he is asked, "Are you determined to employ all your time in the work of God?" What do you think that question means?

4. Pastors are also given these instructions. They have been given to every Methodist pastor since the church began: Be diligent. Never be unemployed. Never be triflingly employed. Never trifle away time, neither spend any more time at any one place than is strictly necessary. Be punctual. Do everything exactly at the time required. How do you feel about these instructions? How does the passage from 1 Peter fit in with these instructions?

Practical Applications

Here are a few exercises to help focus attention on the gift of time. Each of these ideas can help you see how valuable time is; each offers a way to grow in your faithful stewardship. Take time individually to work on the exercise, then share your results with your group.

❖ TIME TITHING — Each and every one of us has the same amount of time given to us: twenty-four hours a day, or 1,440 minutes, to be precise. Sometimes, it seems as if we never have enough time to do everything we want. However, one thing that is extremely important to make time for is our relationship with God.

When we use the term *tithing* we usually refer to money, but what if we made a tithe of our time? The word *tithe* means "one-tenth"; therefore, a tithe of our time would mean that we set aside two hours and twenty-four minutes of each day for God. That would leave us with twenty-one hours and thirty-six minutes to fill with everything else we need and want to do.

What kinds of changes would a time tithe demand in our lives? What would we give up or cut back on? What things would we make sure we had time for? What would the two hours and twenty-four minutes with God be like? How would you spend your time with God? What benefits do you think might come from a time tithe?

❖ **TIME BUDGET** — On a sheet of paper draw two vertical lines, dividing the page into three equal columns. Label the first column ACTIVITIES. Label the middle column IMPORTANCE. Label the last column TIME REQUIRED. Take a few minutes to think of all the things you do during the day: going to school, sleeping, eating, working, playing, studying, relaxing, watching TV, listening to music, talking on the phone, traveling, etc. After you have made as complete a list as possible, number your activities in order of importance in the middle column. Try to be objective. After you have prioritized your activities, calculate how much time you spend each day doing all the things you do. Do you create time for the things that are most important to you? Do the most important things necessarily require the most time? How much of your time is spent on things you feel aren't very important? Does time get wasted? Can you cut out unnecessary uses of time and shift more time to the things most important to you? Can you use time better to accomplish the things most necessary and important in your life?

❖ **TIME SAVER** — Just imagine that each day you could save up to thirty minutes in an account to use whenever you wanted and for whatever you wanted. You could use this time immediately (tack thirty minutes onto the end of each day), or you could save it up. (In three weeks you would have an extra 10 1/2 hours; in a year you could accumulate about 183 hours, or 8 extra days.) How would you use your extra time? What kinds of things would you want to do that you don't have enough time for now? Are there things you could do now during the course of each day that would free up an extra thirty minutes?

Looking Ahead

The next section deals with relationships. You may never have thought of relationships as a gift from God. During the coming week, choose a popular song that best describes your idea of a great relationship.

2 | HAVE A HEART

Lord, make me an instrument of Your peace.
  Where there is hatred, let me sow love;
Where there is injury, pardon;
  Where there is doubt, faith;
Where there is despair, hope;
  Where there is darkness, light;
And where there is sadness, joy.

St. Francis of Assisi

Relationships are tricky things. It has been said that relationships would be easy if *people* weren't involved! People are different. They have different expectations, hopes, needs, desires, likes, opinions, and dreams. But people also need other people. We want people to talk to. We want people to like and respect us. We like attention. We like company. That is the way God made us. In the beginning, when God made Adam and set him in the garden, God saw that it was not good for Adam to be all alone, so God made Eve. When Jesus called disciples and trained them for ministry, he sent them out two by two. Life is much more interesting when there are other people around.

Think of the people that mean the most to you. Realize that each and every one of them is a gift to you from God. Sometimes we might want to give them back; but for the most part, our families, friends, girlfriends, boyfriends, and neighbors are the most valuable gifts we have ever received.

How we treat other people is a good indicator of Christ's place in our lives. The Golden Rule states: "Do unto others as you would have them do unto you." The people God brings into our lives offer us the opportunity to test this rule. It applies equally to people we know well and to those who are strangers. God is very interested in how we manage and appreciate our relationships. Of all the gifts we have been given, perhaps the stewardship of our relationships is the most important.

We don't approach all of our relationships in the same way. We act differently with our parents or brothers and sisters than we do with friends. We act differently with a girlfriend or boyfriend than we do with a teacher or our pastor. We treat our boss differently than we do our grandparents. At times, it feels as if we're a dozen different people. No matter how varied our relationships may be, each one is still very important. The Bible gives a great deal of guidance in how we should act and how we should treat other people. It also challenges us in the ways we relate to God. If we have a good relationship with God, it follows that we will have good relationships with other people. The key is commitment. Good relationships—with God or with other people—take a lot of work and care. Sometimes we take for granted that our relationships will remain constant or will get better, when in fact the only growing, strong relationship is one where we are investing a good deal of time and effort. We need to develop a deep appreciation for our relationships so that we will faithfully nurture and manage them. Relationships are a central stewardship concern.

Dilemmas

#1 Beth knew Slater asked her out so she would help him with his homework, but she really didn't care. Beth was sure he wouldn't dump her once he found out what she was really like. He had a reputation for being a real "user," taking advantage of people for what he could get out of them, then moving on to someone else. It was worth the risk. Slater was so cool, and all of Beth's friends were so jealous that he had asked her out. She had never felt about anyone else the way she felt about Slater. She could change him. She knew she could.

1. How do you think Beth defines a love relationship? How do you think Slater defines one?

2. What possible problems do you see in the future for Beth? For Slater?

3. From the list that follows, choose the words that you think describe Beth. And Slater?

manipulative	lonely	naive
selfish	caring	loving
innocent	shrewd	stupid

4. What advice might you give Beth if she talked to you about her relationship with Slater?

#2 Mr. Fogerty was weird. Everybody in town thought so. Sheila, Alisha, and Vanessa watched him whenever he was around, and they whispered to each other and laughed at the jokes they made at his expense. Secretly, each of the girls felt a little sorry for the old man. He had Parkinson's disease and could hardly control his own movement. The girls didn't really mean to be cruel, but he made them nervous. Not long ago, the rumor had started that he molested children. It upset the whole town, and Mr. Fogerty had almost moved away because of the shame and the suspicion. Alisha and Vanessa had been instrumental in spreading the rumor. They told all their friends what they had heard. Sheila spread the rumor too at first, but when she saw how much damage it did, she stopped. Sometimes she felt like speaking to Mr. Fogerty, but she knew how her friends would make fun of her. It was easier just to whisper and laugh whenever he walked by.

1. Do you think the three girls have a relationship with Mr. Fogerty? If so, what is it? If not, what keeps this situation from being a relationship?

2. Why do Alisha, Sheila, and Vanessa make fun of Mr. Fogerty? Why do they fear him? Why would they spread rumors about someone they don't really know?

3. Do Alisha, Sheila, and Vanessa have any responsibility to care for Mr. Fogerty? Why or why not? In what ways might they care for him?

4. Why is gossip so tempting? Does it matter if the gossip is true or not? An old proverb states, "That which is said, is said forever." Once a reputation is damaged, is there any way to repair it?

#3 David's parents were such geeks. They always tried to stick their noses in his business and tell him what he could and couldn't do. He wasn't a kid, for crying out loud. He wasn't stupid, either. His parents could sure be stupid, though. They didn't understand anything he was going through. Most of their ideas were from the Stone Age. They spent all their time worrying that he might be on drugs or having sex or doing something illegal. They didn't trust him at all. It felt as if all they ever wanted to do was ground him for the dumbest things. As soon as he was old enough, David was going to move out and never look back. They would be sorry they treated him like a jerk. Once he was gone, he would be gone for good.

1. How would you say that David relates to his parents? How do his parents relate to David?

2. What elements might be missing from David's relationship with his parents? Do you think David understands his parents any better than they understand him?

3. Describe how you think David would rather be treated by his parents. What advice would you give David's parents about how to better relate to him? What would you tell David about the way he relates to his mom and dad?

4. Do you think David loves his parents? Do you think his parents love David? Why or why not?

Biblical Reflections

PRAYER: God of the whole human family, we thank you for making us who we are. We thank you for the differences in personality that make life both interesting and frustrating. We thank you for people who are like us and for those who are very different. Help us remember that we are all created in your image. Let unity be our desire, and help us to make new friends—to be joined as brothers and sisters. Show us that we are the most precious gift to one another that you have ever given, with the exception of your own Son. Make us value the gift that we are and teach us to be good stewards of all our relationships. We ask your blessing in Jesus' holy name. Amen.

A friend is a gift you give yourself.

Robert Louis Stevenson

1 Corinthians 13:1-8*a*   Philippians 2:1-4

1. These two passages offer us some guidelines for the way we relate
    to others. In your own words, what would you say are the most
    important qualities we need to bring to our relationships?

2. What makes it difficult to consider the needs and wants of others
    as more important than your own wants and needs? Why should
    we have to make sacrifices so other people can get what they
    want?

3. Using Paul's definitions of love, select people from the following
    list who are easiest to love. Select those who are difficult to love.
    What makes it easy to love some people and difficult to love others?

mother	father	boyfriend/girlfriend
teacher	friend	neighbor
child	older people	stranger
foreigner	grandparent	aunt/uncle
cousin	brother/sister	pastor/youth leader

4. From the two passages you read, make a list of the things that
    are good in your relationships and a list of the things that need
    improvement. What is the greatest strength or good quality
    that you bring to your relationships?

Luke 6:27-36   James 2:19   Matthew 25:31-46

1. To what kinds of people do you tend to show partiality? What kinds of things impress you most about people? Do you tend to focus more on what people have, how they act, or what they believe?

2. Loving your enemy seems like a strange thing to do. Why is it hard to love enemies and people we don't like? What makes people enemies in the first place? Why should we have to love our enemies when they refuse to love us?

3. An anonymous leader of the early Christian church encouraged his students to say to themselves whenever they met a stranger, "I would like the Christ that is in me to meet the Christ that is in you, that we might become brothers." How would your opinion of others change if you believed that all people carried Christ within them?

4. Once we learn to appreciate even our enemies, in what ways do we become managers of our relationships? Explain what you think the stewardship of relationships means.

Ephesians 4:25-32   Colossians 3:5-17

1. Make a list of do's and don'ts that Paul recommends we use in the way we relate to God and to one another. Compare the instruction in Colossians to that in Ephesians. Is there anything you would add to the list?

2. What earthly qualities do you need to put to death in your life? Which qualities do you need to put on? Which of the negative qualities do the most to harm relationships? Which good qualities do the most to strengthen relationships?

3. Forgiveness is a big issue in relationships, and it is a big issue in the Bible. The Lord's Prayer states: "Forgive us our trespasses as we forgive those who trespass against us." Why is it so important to be able to forgive and to be forgiven in our relationships? Whom is it easiest to forgive? Whom is it hardest to forgive? How do you deal with someone who won't forgive you?

Practical Applications

❖ **PERFECT FRIEND** — On a sheet of paper, list all the qualities you feel a perfect friend would have. Also note the qualities that he or she should definitely not have. In a group, compare your list with those of other people in the group. What are the potential problems with finding someone who fits your list exactly? If you could have only three of your good qualities in a friend, and you had to have one of the qualities that you definitely do not want, which would they be?

❖ **SAY SO!** — In our lives we make many friends and acquaintances, but often we don't let people know how special they are to us. Make three lists. The first is a list of all your current friends and people you really care about. The second list includes people you care about that you haven't seen for awhile. The third is a list of acquaintances— people you don't know well. Choose a couple of people from each list and write them a note or a letter. This is good stewardship of our relationships. It puts us in touch and allows us to use wisely one of our most valuable gifts: communication. The content of the note should be a simple "I like you. I'm glad to know you. Thank you for being a friend." This is especially meaningful for the people on your second list with whom you have fallen out of touch. A note to a former friend, teacher, neighbor, whomever, may be the best thing that happens to them the day they receive it. It is a small act that can do a great deal to encourage someone else. Strong relationships are built on this kind of caring stewardship. If you care about somebody, say so!

❖ **PRAYER PROJECTION** — It's impossible not to care about somebody for whom you are praying. Prayer for another person connects us in a very special way to that other person, even to a stranger. In a way, this is a kind of game, but it's a serious spiritual exercise as well. Wherever you are, at any time of day, start "zapping" people with prayers. You see somebody who looks sad. Zap! Pray that God might brighten that person's day. You run into a grouchy sales clerk. Blam! Bounce a prayer for joy his way. See the many faces of people in too big a hurry? Calm them down with a "chill out" prayer. Walk down the sidewalk, ride down the street, sit in a classroom, and send prayers out at everyone you see. It makes you notice people more, it makes you care about people more, and it reminds you that you are God's partner in the sacred stewardship of relationships. Projecting prayers at people has startling effects, too. Some people don't know what's happening exactly, but they know something's up. Praying for others may open the door to some great new friendships. The fifth chapter of James reminds us that the prayer of one truly concerned Christian can change lives. You won't know until you try. Use the power. "Zap" somebody soon.

Looking Ahead

Next week we will begin looking at money and possessions and what it means to be faithful stewards of them. Watch for TV commercials, magazine ads, and radio promos that tell us we need *things* to make us happy, or popular, or healthy. Notice how they make us feel dissatisfied with what we have so that we want something new or different in order to be happy. Think about the things that really make you happy and what your life would be like without them.

> *Often people attempt to live their lives backwards;*
> *they try to have more things, or more money, in order*
> *to do more of what they want, so they will be happier.*
> *The way it actually works is the reverse. You must first*
> *be who you really are, then do what you need to do,*
> *in order to have what you really want.*
>
> Margaret Young
> *LIFE 101**

---

* From *LIFE 101: Everything We Wish We Had Learned About Life in School—But Didn't* by Peter McWilliams and John-Roger, published by Prelude Press, 8159 Santa Monica Boulevard, Los Angeles, CA 90046, **1-800-LIFE-101**. Used by permission.

3 | STUFF!

There are two things to aim at in life: first, to get what you want; and after that, to enjoy it. Only the wisest of humankind achieve the second.

Logan Pearsall Smith
*Wealth 101**

A young mother grew concerned when she realized she hadn't heard a peep out of her four-year-old son. She began a search of the house, and as she approached his bedroom, she heard him laugh with pleasure. Opening his door, the woman was momentarily stunned. Her son sat atop a large pile of books, toys, clothes, stuffed animals, blankets, pillows, and a variety of other items. Looking around the room, she saw that not one possession remained in place on any shelf, in any drawer, in any closet, or on any piece of furniture. As the young child caught sight of his mother, he happily shouted, "Mom, look at all my stuff!"

As George Carlin says, we live in a society of "stuff." A common attitude is, the more stuff the better. A bumper sticker proclaims, "Whoever dies with the most toys wins." Many people dedicate their lives to the accumulation of more and more stuff. We love stuff. Stuff is fun. And the most important and necessary ingredient in the pursuit of stuff is money. As the emcee sings in *Cabaret*, money makes the world go 'round. There are very few things that can be accomplished in our world without money. Money gives us the freedom to buy stuff, and no matter how much stuff we have, there is

---

* From *Wealth 101: Wealth Is Much More Than Money* by Peter McWilliams and Roger-John, published by Prelude Press, 8159 Santa Monica Boulevard, Los Angeles, CA 90046, **1-800-LIFE-101.** Used by permission.

always more stuff to want. For many people, making money and buying stuff is what gives their life meaning.

Liking money and possessions is not wrong unless, of course, they become the most important things in our lives. God gives us our lives as a gift and intends that we should enjoy the gift. God gives us the creativity to dream all kinds of good things, places untold resources at our disposal, and gives each individual a personality that is defined by tastes, preferences, and desires. It would be cruel of God to create people with all of these characteristics, and then forbid them to enjoy anything. Faithful stewardship does not mean "doing without"; it means "doing with integrity." Management and appreciation are at the heart of stewardship. A good manager keeps things in balance. Money and all the goodies it can buy are fine, so long as they are kept in proper perspective with the rest of our lives. Sometimes, though, we expect our possessions to fulfill us and make us happy; then we're disappointed when they can't do that. What develops then is an insatiable hunger for "more and better"—more clothes, more games, more CDs, better shoes, better stereos, better cars. Somewhere inside our heads the idea pops up that if we can just get enough, then we'll be happy. Until we learn to be happy with what we've got, we soon find that we never have enough. We want more.

The key to good stewardship of our money and things has nothing to do with getting rid of what we have, but learning to find satisfaction with less. When we lower our sights on what defines "enough," we reach it faster. When we develop gratitude and appreciation to God for the things we already have, we find that we really don't think about getting more. Sometimes, in order to realize how fortunate we are, we need to look at the world around us and to take an inventory of all we have that the majority of the world doesn't. This applies not only to material possessions, but also to less tangible things, such as our rights and freedoms.

It's okay to have favorite possessions. The things we like make our lives richer, and they give us comfort, enjoyment, satisfaction, and, sometimes, security. It's okay to save money for special things— and even to be extravagant at times. The important thing to remember is that our "stuff" can only do so much for us. There are very few things in life that we can't learn to do without, so if we can seek to place less value on our things, then we will not be so anxious about having them.

There are some Native American tribes that hold to an ideal that nothing is truly owned, but all is merely borrowed, placed in our possession to use for awhile until the time comes for it to pass on. No land titles change hands, for land cannot be owned. Cars and homes are left unlocked, because nothing can be stolen from a person who doesn't own anything. Farm produce is available to any person who comes along, and in bad weather any person is welcome to find shelter in the nearest dwelling. Ownership is not vital to a person's identity.

As stewards, we do not see ourselves as owners, but as caretakers. We manage, and we are given the privilege of enjoying whatever is in our care. What a freeing way of thinking! We don't have to hold tightly to the things we have. We don't have to defend and protect "our property." Sharing becomes the new rule, and needing to "own" things becomes less important. We find it increasingly impossible to worship things, and we find more time to be thankful to God. Keeping our priorities straight is a vital element of good Christian stewardship.

Dilemmas

#1 Jonathan's grandfather had set up a trust for his college education when Jonathan was just five years old. Various members of the family had deposited small amounts of money into the trust over the years, and now it held over $11,000. College was still two years away, though, and Jonathan was ready to get a car. His dad kept telling him that he couldn't afford a car, but Jonathan told him that he could use the trust money. His father said he couldn't touch that money for anything but college, but that seemed unfair to Jonathan. He felt that he should be able to decide how his money would be spent. He needed a car for school and work, and, besides, he could make enough money in two years to replace the money in the trust fund. The car was an immediate need; college was a long way off. The money belonged to him anyway, so if that's the way he wanted to spend it, nobody should be able to tell him otherwise.

1. What stewardship issues (management and appreciation) do you see in this story?

2. In your opinion, to whom does the money belong? How should decisions about its use be made?

3. How would you try to resolve the conflict between Jonathan and his dad if you were Jonathan? His dad?

4. It's often difficult to set priorities for spending money when some things we want are immediate, and other things are far off in the future. How can we keep immediate wants in perspective when other equally important things make us wait?

#2 Ricki never had any money. It was embarrassing. His friends always seemed to have more than he did. They asked him to go to the arcade or to the mall or to the movies, and he always had to come up with some lame excuse. He got caught stealing once, just because he wanted to get a tape like the one all his friends were listening to. His mom didn't seem to care. She told him that some people had and some people didn't—and right now Ricki's family didn't! Life wasn't fair. While his friends went out, Ricki had to stay home and watch TV. When the guys went out to McDonald's, he had to microwave his own dinner while his mom worked late. When they went out to play basketball, he wore year-old shoes, while all his friends wore new shoes. His best friend Jason just got a new CD player and all Ricki had was his brother's old Walkman. It felt like everybody else got good, new stuff but him.

1. Is Ricki's real problem that he doesn't have money? If so, what can he do about it? If not, what are the real issues? What can he do about them?

2. There is an old saying, "You would gripe if you were hung with a new rope." It means that some people are incapable of seeing any good in a situation. In what ways is Ricki blind to the good in his situation?

3. In this story, why are money and things so important to Ricki? What would you say to Ricki if he were your friend and you knew he felt the way he does?

4. How would Ricki's life be changed if he had all the things his friends had? In what ways would Ricki's feelings change if he had more money? Are there other problems that Ricki is dealing with that more money won't solve? What are they?

#3 Dana was so mad. She had loaned her favorite shirt to her friend Renee, and when it came back, it had a stain on it. Renee had just shrugged her shoulders and said, "Sorry," then gone home. She couldn't have cared less! The shirt had cost $40, and now it was a rag. The shirt itself didn't mean that much, but Renee's attitude hurt. How would Renee like it if Dana ruined *her* favorite clothes? She wouldn't like it at all. How could somebody borrow something from someone else and then not take care of what they borrowed? Renee didn't care about the friendship at all; she just wanted to borrow the shirt. If she was any kind of friend, she would offer to buy Dana a new one. Dana thought it would serve Renee right if she sent her a bill.

1. In what ways is Dana justified in her reaction? In what ways is Dana getting carried away?

2. This story reveals more than just how two people feel about possessions. It shows how they value one another. Where do you see instances of good stewardship of possessions? Bad stewardship of possessions? Where do you see good stewardship of friendship? Bad stewardship of friendship?

3. Based on your observation of the situation from Dana's perspective, how would you say Dana and Renee prioritize friendship and possessions? Is losing a thing ever more important than keeping a friendship?

4. How is "respect" a crucial element of stewardship?

Biblical Reflections

PRAYER: Gracious God, giver of all good things, help us remember that it is impossible to have more than one Lord. Make certain that we never value "things" more highly than we value you or our neighbor. Teach us to be giving, sharing, caring people, who take what we have and enjoy it—but not at the expense of another human being. Turn our attention away from the things we lack, open our eyes to see the things we have, and make us truly thankful. Speak to us through your holy Word that we might gain understanding of what it means to be good stewards of money and possessions. We pray in Jesus' name. Amen.

Read the following passages of scripture, and answer the subsequent questions:

Matthew 25:14-30   Luke 12:22-34

1. In the Matthew parable, the amount of money made is not the issue. If God is not interested in how well we do financially, then what is God interested in? Why is God so angry with the steward who buried his talent in the ground? (A talent is a weight measure. A talent of silver was equal to approximately fifteen years' wages in the time of Jesus.)

2. Faith is a big part of stewardship. To manage and to appreciate money without anxiety, we need to develop a great deal of faith. How do the servants in the Matthew passage display their faith? What does the Luke passage say about how God expects stewards to behave?

3. If we are not to be concerned with our own material needs, then what does God expect our focus to be?

4. According to the passages in Matthew and Luke, which of the following terms do you feel best describe what money is?

power	a tool	important
necessary	anxiety-producing	fun
a stumbling block	holy	dangerous
confusing	valuable	evil

Luke 18:18-30   Mark 12:41-44

1. The stewardship of money requires not only appreciation and management, but also a clear sense of its purpose. Money is a means to an end, rather than an end in itself. It is a tool by which we can accomplish many things. Therefore, the way we spend money and where we use it are as important as how we manage it. In these passages, how do the main characters differ in the way they use their money? What makes the rich ruler sad when Jesus tells him what to do?

2. What is it that makes the widow's gift so special? In the case of the rich young ruler, is it the amount of money he has to give away or his reluctance to give it that is the main problem? What makes it hard for people to give money away? Why wouldn't it be acceptable for the rich young ruler to give away *some* of his money instead of *all* of it?

3. The Bible says that we cannot worship two masters: God and money. We are always pulled in two directions. If money is too important to us, how can it damage our relationship with God?

4. The rich young ruler was obedient to the commandments and he understood the law. He was, in fact, a good man. If he was such a good person, why couldn't he keep his money and continue to live the way he always had? Where was the rich ruler's heart—with God or with money? How can we tell?

2 Corinthians 8:12-15; 9:6-15   Exodus 36:2-7

1. Generosity is a quality of the Christian steward. Giving for the sake of giving is not the point, though, because there are many ways to give generously that are foolish and wasteful. The steward of God is entrusted with money and possessions to manage for the good of all people. If we are given a blessing from God, it is a blessing that we are expected to share with others. How much of what we have do you think God expects us to share with others?

2. Paul says that the Lord loves a cheerful giver. When we give, do we give cheerfully? Does the amount of money we have make a difference in our ability to give it cheerfully? What other things influence our ability to give cheerfully besides the amount of money we have?

3. In the Exodus story, Moses collected offerings of money and possessions with which to build a sanctuary. The people were so enthusiastic in their giving (and they were not wealthy people, either), that they gave too much! In our world, do you think it would be possible for so much money to be given that no more money would be needed? Can we ever give too much? What things besides money do we need to give in order to honor God?

Giving can take hold of a person like a fever. There is great joy and satisfaction in giving. In fact, we often feel even more fortunate and wealthy when we give things away than we feel by keeping them. The entire biblical witness testifies to the giving nature of God. God gives because giving is a good thing, and within the act of giving is incredible joy and good feeling. God calls us to share in the joy and excitement of giving.

The Bible has so much to say on the subject of money and possessions. Jesus deals with the topic of money more than any other topic, with the exception of the kingdom of God. Money has the power to do great good—and to do great damage. In 1 Timothy 6:10, Paul teaches that the love of money is the root of all human evil. The relationship we have with money and with all the stuff it can buy cannot help but affect the relationship we have with God. We must be good and generous stewards of our money and possessions, or our possessions just might possess us.

Practical Applications

❖ "HALVES" AND HAVE NOTS — We spend a lot of money on things we don't really need, or at least on things we don't need as much of. A good way to see just how much money we spend on little goodies is to spend half as much. Here's a way to do it. Set up a jar or a bank in a place where you will see it often. Then, whenever you buy a soda or a snack, whenever you rent a video or play an arcade game, whenever you go out for pizza or to the mall, match the amount you spend with an equal amount in the jar or bank. Do this for two weeks, then total up what is in the jar. Don't cheat and dip into the jar whenever money gets tight. Having half as much money to spend forces you to manage wisely—the first element of stewardship. Second, as you sacrifice things you are used to, you will grow to appreciate how lucky you are to have them. Then—and this is the most important part of this experiment—seriously reflect on how much you really gave up by cutting your spending in half. Look at what you have left. It's probably more than you thought you would have. Reflect for a moment on Paul's instruction in 2 Corinthians about sharing from your abundance that there might be equality. Think of a way your money could be used to do something good and meaningful. Your church may have suggestions about where your money might go to help someone who has less than you do. This is another important element of the stewardship of money—using this gift in a charitable and compassionate way. To share from your possessions is to extend the love of Christ in the world. In this way, you sacrifice a little, you still get to enjoy the things you like, and you get the good feeling of doing something for others.

❖ THREE-MINUTE MILLIONAIRE — You have exactly three minutes to figure out how you would dispose of a million dollars if it was handed to you. You have three main ways to divide the money: to spend it on stuff, to save and invest it, and to give it away. Be ready to explain why you use the money the way you do. *Hint:* Do not take this million and bury it in the ground!

❖ FOR WHAT IT'S WORTH — Often we spend so much of ourselves making money that we don't get good value for it when we spend it. What takes us weeks to earn may be gone in a few minutes. A week's allowance can get sucked down the slot of a video game. A paycheck may not survive one trip to the mall. One date can wipe us out for two weeks. Is what we get worth what we spend?

On a sheet of paper, draw a table similar to the one on page 30. List all the things you spend money on in the first column, list how much the things cost in the second column, write down what gives you the most satisfaction in the third column, and place a + or − in the final column to indicate whether or not you feel that the satisfaction was greater or less than what it cost. For example: You go to the mall and spend $25. The real fun of the day is being with your friends. In the first column you would put "mall trip," the second column would say "$25," the third would read "being with friends," and the fourth would register a + if you thought the value you got for your $25 was worth it, a − if you wish you hadn't spent that much money. Once the chart is complete, ask yourself the following questions:

How would I have felt if I had spent less money? Would I have enjoyed myself less? Many times we think we need to buy or spend something in order to have fun, when what is truly fun has very little to do with spending money. Sometimes we spend money more out of habit than out of need or desire.

Stuff	Cost	Satisfaction	+/−

Looking Ahead

The fourth section deals with our stewardship of the earth. During the course of the week, look for ways that caring for our planet has become popular. How is this talked about on TV? What is being done in your community to take seriously our responsibility to be stewards of creation?

4 | CHOOSE LIFE!

My mother told me, "If there's a mess, clean it up!
It don't matter who made it. It don't matter when,
why, or how it was made. If it's there, it needs to
be cleaned up. Grab a mop, rag, or broom—
whatever it takes. You're not just doin' it for you,
but for the next person to come along, too."

Anonymous

It doesn't take a rocket scientist to take a look at our world and see that something is terribly wrong. The ozone layer is breaking up, water is unsafe to drink, deserts are spreading, pollution is growing, millions of people are starving, wars break out between countries, and mini-wars of violence break out in our own streets. Innocent people are shot down, children are abused, the elderly are abandoned, and suicide is a daily result of many people's despair. "Behold a broken world," says a hymn by Timothy Dudley-Smith (*The United Methodist Hymnal*, No. 426), and indeed, the time has come for faithful stewards of God to take serious note of the world's condition. Is this really what God intended?

The first great responsibility God ever placed into the hands of humankind was to take care of all that had been created. Adam and Eve were given "dominion" over all the plants and trees, animals, birds, and fish. This dominion gave them the right to decide which creatures would live and die, which plants could be uprooted and replanted, and the awesome task of giving everything a name. God gave Adam and Eve authority—the right to rule in God's place. This did not mean, however, that Adam and Eve could do anything they wanted. Unfortunately, over the centuries, many people have chosen that interpretation of *dominion*.

A steward is given power and authority, the right to manage and make decisions, but the choices a steward makes should always reflect the will and values of the true owner. A steward represents a master. God trusts us to make godlike decisions. To do less is simply bad stewardship.

Likewise, the master entrusts the steward with possessions with the expectation that those possessions will be returned in at least as good a condition as they started out. In fact, the steward has the responsibility to return them in even better condition. Think of the passage in Matthew 25 where the master entrusted his stewards with the talents. Good and faithful stewards took the talents placed in their care and, through creativity and skill, they improved them. God wants us to do the best with what we have been given—not the worst. We can feel free to *use* the gifts, but we should never feel free to use them *up*. Whatever God entrusts to us is given not merely for our own use, but for the benefit and well-being of others as well.

Human beings have lived happily on the planet for a long time, enjoying its resources and not taking too much notice of the problems they were creating. It appeared that there would always be enough clean air, fresh water, and safe and fertile land to live on. No one gave any thought to running out of air, water, or land. In the last fifty years, however, these concerns have come to people's attention. With the invention of television and all of the technological advances in communications in the past few decades, we now see the rest of the world on a regular basis. We realize that there are millions of starving and sick people in the world. We know about rainforests and apartheid and overpopulation. We see the problems caused by events in Chernobyl and Bophar and Iraq. We begin to feel that our planet isn't so huge after all, that we are a global community, and that what affects a few people really affects many.

We want to do something, but the problems are so big! We are overwhelmed by the proportions of our global dilemmas. We think about what we can do to make a difference, and we end up shrugging our shoulders and turning our attention to something easier to handle, while a small voice in the back of our minds tells us that ignoring these things won't make them go away. What should we be doing?

What is the role of the Christian steward in the face of such widespread problems? As we look ahead to the future, the issues of environmental and social stewardship loom largest of all. We need God's guidance and strength more than ever if we are to respond faithfully to this challenge.

Dilemmas

#1 Michael thought the church people were crazy. The missions committee had set aside a special day of prayer, fasting, and letter writing in solidarity with all the homeless and hungry people in the world. What a waste of time! Those people didn't need symbolic acts and prayers. What they needed were places to live and food to eat. It would make a lot more sense for the congregation to raise money or to volunteer to work in soup kitchens and shelters. It seemed as if every time there was a problem in the world, the church gathered to pray and think about it instead of really *doing* anything. What good would it do some hungry person for Michael to go without food? How could praying produce a home for a homeless person? It just didn't make any sense at all.

1. Answer Michael's questions for him. What possible good does it do a hungry person when we fast? How might prayer help a homeless person? How do you feel about Michael's assessment that the church doesn't do anything to deal with real problems?

2. What is the church's responsibility to address issues such as hunger and homelessness?

3. From the list on the following page, choose the three activities you feel are most important for the church to engage in to address issues such as homelessness and hunger.

prayer   service projects   fund-raising events
fasting   training missionaries   giving money to missions
education   hosting homeless people   donating food and clothing

Can you add other things to this list that the church should be doing?

#2 Recycling was such a chore. Jason used to like collecting cans when he got paid for it, and he always had fun when the Scouts had a paper drive, but now everybody had to recycle everything, and no one got paid extra for it. It was so much easier throwing everything into one garbage bag and hauling it out to the street. Let the garbage collectors sort it out—it's their job. Jason couldn't figure out what good recycling was really going to accomplish. Most things couldn't be recycled, and products made from recycled materials eventually were dumped in landfills anyway. Why didn't they just burn it? Then it would be out of everybody's way. Or maybe they could load it into rockets and shoot it into space. Garbage shouldn't be such a big issue. Just bury it. And as far as recycling went, the amount of trash Jason's family produced wasn't going to ruin the environment. Let the *real* polluters recycle.

1. Do you find any flaws in Jason's reasoning? What are they? What good points does Jason make?

2. Whose responsibility is it to recycle? What measures need to be taken to ensure that big companies and industries take environmental issues seriously? How can we promote the need for recycling in homes, schools, churches, and local businesses?

3. What are the stewardship issues in the story? In what ways is Jason dealing with these issues? What does Jason lack in order to be a good steward?

#3 Who would have thought that raising money for the hungry and homeless could be so much fun? What had started out as a simple suggestion had turned into a wonderful time for the whole class. Mr. Burroughs had told a story about a clinic that had been started years before by a nun who gathered pennies off the street and saved them in buckets and jars. When the story was publicized through the media, thousands of people sent millions of pennies to her to support her work. Great things were accomplished—one penny at a time. Curt suggested that the class begin collecting pennies for the homeless and hungry in their city. Everyone thought it would be a great idea, then Kayla challenged the guys in the class by saying that the girls could collect more than they could. It became a contest. For weeks, both guys and girls rounded up all the change they could find. Local businesses and individuals heard of the contest and began sending cash and checks to the class. At the end of ten weeks, over $2,000 had been raised . . . one penny at a time.

1. What insights does this story offer about the difficulty or ease with which we can try to make a difference in dealing with social problems?

2. How does this story challenge our thinking about making a "significant contribution" to justice issues in our world?

3. What ingredients helped make this penny challenge a successful event?

Biblical Reflections

PRAYER: Creating and loving God, fill us with an awesome respect for all the good things you have made. Remind us that our planet has been put in our hands as a sacred trust. You watch carefully to see how we treat the earth, the animals, and each other. You created the earth to be a paradise, and by your guiding Spirit you encourage us to dedicate ourselves to reclaiming the peaceful garden you originally intended. Grant us the wisdom to know what must be done, then grant us the strength and conviction to make it happen. Enable us to be good stewards of all that you have made, we humbly pray in the name of Jesus Christ. Amen.

Read the following passages of scripture and answer the subsequent questions:

Psalm 24:1-2   Genesis 1:1-31

1. What do these passages tell us about the way God hopes the earth will be treated?

2. Reflect on the story of creation. What are some of the ways the world has changed since its creation? How have we improved upon the earth God created? What have we spoiled?

3. We live in an age of astounding technological advancement and scientific achievement. How can we enjoy the benefits of our human accomplishment and, at the same time, affirm the world as God created it?

4. Do you think God expected human beings to treat the world the way they have? Why or why not?

Isaiah 40:12-31   Job 38:1-38

1. We sometimes think we own things, when in fact God is the only
    true owner of everything. God created every thing in existence;
    nothing that men and women have fashioned has been "created"
    by them. We merely take what God gives and we make things
    with it. What do we owe to God for all that God has given us?
    How do we find a balance between doing what *we* want with
    God's creation and making sure we also do what *God* wants?

2. What difference does it make for us to commit to be good stew-
    ards of the earth and our communities, when the vast majority of
    people don't share our commitment? What is the best way to
    help people realize the problems we face if we continue to trash
    the planet?

3. In what ways are we challenged to change our behavior, knowing
    that we don't own the earth but are tending it for God? What
    new responsibilities do we have to animals, fish, birds, plants,
    trees, etc.? How are we challenged concerning the way we care
    for people who are in need?

Micah 6:6-8   Luke 10:25-37

1. How are justice, kindness, and humility dimensions of stewardship?

2. What determines whether a person deserves help? How can we
    develop the ability to know when it is right for us to help and
    when it is foolish or wrong?

3. From the list that follows, divide the qualities that strengthen stewardship from the qualities that weaken stewardship:

obedience	compassion	prejudice
justice	piety	kindness
charity	righteousness	judgment
fear	contempt	humility

    Could any of these terms swing both ways—sometimes strengths, sometimes weaknesses?

    Stewardship of the earth means more than just being environmentally aware and concerned. We are also stewards of the inhabitants of our planet as it circles through space. That means stewards are also politically, socially, and economically aware. There is so much injustice in the world, and only through facing the problems honestly will we ever be moved to take only our fair share—and nothing more. Turning off the TV when images from South Africa, India, and Central America invade our homes is not good stewardship. Striving to feel what the suffering feel, to fear what the oppressed fear, to understand what the less fortunate think—these are important parts of our Christian stewardship. Good stewardship is more than just acknowledging the problems, however. To be effective, we must not only assess the damage in our world, but also grasp the beauty and goodness that exist on our planet. We are caretakers of hope and encouragement, and our responsibility to the poor and oppressed in the world requires that we share "good news."

    The Bible only takes us so far. It helps us see what God intends, but it is up to us to move out into our communities and into the world to put these teachings into action. Our churches should be "filling stations," equipping us to reach out to those who need the blessing and touch of Christ. This is a great challenge—the challenge that makes stewardship one of the most important tasks of the church and of each individual believer.

Practical Applications

❖ EDUCATION EVENT — The best way to learn is to teach. Suppose you were going to work with your youth group (or any group) to present an environmental stewardship program at your church. How would you do it? What materials would you need? Would you bring in speakers from the outside? Who would they be? Where would you go for the information you would need to run the program? Does the church have any resources you could draw from? Your community? What topics would you address? Where would this event take place? How would you make it dramatic enough so that people would take note? Take time to design your program, then pursue it and do it. Make this more than an exercise. Make it an event!

❖ WASTE REDUCTION — Draw a line down the center of a sheet of paper. On one side, list all the ways you are wasteful. On the other side, list all the ways you conserve resources and avoid waste. Trace your whole day from the time you get up to the time you go to bed. Think of times you use water, food, paper, gasoline, electricity, plastic, chemicals, and anything else you want to consider. Try to be specific about all the ways you waste or conserve. It's very hard to change our behavior if we're not aware of our bad habits. Likewise, we are often unaware of our own good habits. Share your list with everyone else in the group. Other people may remind you of something you overlooked in your own life. Now, choose one or two waste areas and make a commitment to cut back on waste in those areas. Target one or two ways you might begin to conserve. Ask everyone to write their commitment on a large sheet of paper and sign it. Make a copy of these waste reduction and conservation covenants for everyone in the group. As good stewards, hold one another accountable to cut back on waste.

❖ FASTING — Fasting is not a familiar practice in our society, except as a way to lose weight quickly. Fasting is a spiritual discipline that helps us acknowledge our dependence on God, to be reminded of how lucky we are to have a full stomach most of the time, and to make us more compassionate as we experience in a very small way what the majority of our global neighbors experience every single day. When we fast, we find our ideas and attitudes changing. We find that we don't want others to suffer like that. We learn that we don't need as much as we thought we did. And we learn to be much more appreciative of the things we have instead of always wanting what we don't have. Fasting puts us in touch with who we really are and what we really feel.

The best way to fast is "noon to noon." Following a light snack at 11:30 AM, drink a couple of glasses of water. About mid-afternoon you will feel hungry. You aren't really hungry, but your stomach is in the habit of having food in it, so it kicks up a fuss. Ignore it. Use the time when you are usually eating dinner to talk with your family or to spend some quiet time with God. Here is where it gets a little tough. Your stomach is going to know that you're ignoring it, so it will get mad at you. You will most likely want to break your fast as the sun goes down and the night stretches on. Whenever the pangs of hunger set in, grit your teeth, close your eyes, and pray, "Thank you, God, for all you provide—for food and shelter and all good things. Thank you that I am fortunate enough not to feel this way often. Help me to be more caring for those who are in need. Amen." (Any other prayer of gratitude will do.) Your body will readjust itself overnight, and hunger will not be so great in the morning. However, as time goes by, the hunger will be great. Whenever hunger strikes, drink water. Make sure you keep plenty of water in your system; it makes fasting much easier. At lunchtime, have something light to break the fast—no cheeseburgers or pizza! If you fast regularly, you will find that you develop a greater stewardship sensitivity and that you turn more frequently to God for strength and support. Fasting may be a lost art in our church, but it is one well worth reviving.

CONCLUSION

What choice do we have? If we want to be Christians, we really don't have much of a choice: We must be stewards! That is part of what it means to be a Christian. The Bible makes it clear that we have been entrusted with gifts from God, and that God wants us to use them wisely and well. Jesus instructed his followers, "Strive first for the kingdom of God and his righteousness, and all these things will be given unto you as well" (Matt. 6:3). As we zero in on the kingdom, we realize that the only way to find it in this world is to become obedient to the call to faithful stewardship. God gives us our life as a gift, not as a curse. God's greatest intention is that we might be the very best we can be—to reach our full potential and to know joy. God's name is written upon each of our hearts. We belong to the Lord. In gratitude and appreciation, we joyfully care for everything that we have been given—for each hour of every day, for the people who make our lives special and unique, for the great stuff we have to use and to enjoy, and for the home, community, and world in which we live. We have so much, if we only take time to see it.

There is one more element of faithful Christian stewardship that needs to be underlined. This element has been a part of each section we have explored, yet it is so obvious that we might miss it. The best way to describe this element is to call it "the ability to get out of the way."

It is important to remember that, historically, a steward is also a servant. Look at the story of Joseph in Genesis 41:37. Joseph, in Egypt, was a servant of Pharaoh, yet he rose to be almost as powerful as Pharaoh himself in the role of chief steward. A servant must adopt an attitude of humility and grace, putting the needs and wants of others ahead of his or her own. A servant respects even those unworthy of respect, is kind to those who in no way warrant kindness, and is patient with the most irritating and annoying people imaginable.

Unless the servant adopts these attitudes freely, servanthood quickly becomes slavery.

Our culture does not support an attitude of servanthood. We live in a "stand on your own two feet, don't let anybody push you around, you gotta look out for number one, God helps those who help themselves" kind of culture. A true steward, one who accepts the identity of a servant, is just asking to be taken advantage of. So what? Jesus himself was mocked and persecuted, laughed at and scorned. He didn't seem to mind. The reason Jesus didn't care what others thought was that he knew in his heart who God wanted him to be, and he gave everything he had to live up to that expectation. Jesus could serve because he was called to serve. Jesus could teach and preach because he knew he was called to teach and preach. Jesus could even die upon the cross for our salvation because he knew it was the right thing to do.

Take a look at these two passages of scripture:

John 13:1-20   Philippians 2:5-11

Jesus provides us with a powerful model of stewardship. One woman defines stewardship as "doing the job that needs to be done with the basic tools God gives you." Some of the basic tools we all share are kindness, encouragement, sympathy, a sense of humor, concern, a desire to help, and the ability to love. When we put these tools to good use, chances are that we are being fairly good stewards.

Jesus has been called the "chief steward among stewards," and we do well to follow his example. We may never be perfect as Jesus was perfect, but we can say yes to the call that God has offered us: to be faithful Christian stewards of all the good gifts we have been given.

The hymn, "Here I Am, Lord" in *The United Methodist Hymnal* offers us both a sense of God's purpose in the world and the challenge to answer the call. Read the words to this hymn on the following page, and reflect on their meaning. God calls, and we have a choice to make.

HERE I AM, LORD

I, the Lord of sea and sky, I have heard my people cry.
All who dwell in dark and sin my hand will save.
I who made the stars of night, I will make their darkness bright.
Who will bear my light to them? Whom shall I send?

Here I am, Lord.
Is it I, Lord?
I have heard you calling in the night.
I will go, Lord,
if you lead me.
I will hold your people in my heart.

I, the Lord of snow and rain, I have borne my people's pain.
I have wept for love of them. They turn away.
I will break their hearts of stone, give them hearts for love alone.
I will speak my word to them. Whom shall I send?

Here I am, Lord.
Is it I, Lord?
I have heard you calling in the night.
I will go, Lord,
if you lead me.
I will hold your people in my heart.

I, the Lord of wind and flame, I will tend the poor and lame,
I will set a feast for them. My hand will save.
Finest bread I will provide till their hearts be satisfied.
I will give my life to them. Whom shall I send?

Here I am, Lord.
Is it I, Lord?
I have heard you calling in the night.
I will go, Lord,
if you lead me.
I will hold your people in my heart.

WORDS: Dan Schutte, 1981 (Isa. 6:8)
MUSIC: Dan Schutte, 1981; adapt. by Carlton R. Young, 1988
From *The United Methodist Hymnal*, No. 593 (Nashville: The United Methodist Publishing
House, 1989). Used by permission.

GROUP HELPS

Here are a few supplemental suggestions of ways to deal with the stewardship issues in this study. These ideas can be incorporated into longer youth group gatherings, Sunday school classes where the sections are dealt with over a number of weeks, or, especially, retreat settings. These supplemental ideas can also be used by individuals working their way through the book. These ideas require no special expertise or biblical knowledge; they are included to challenge thinking and for personal reflection.

Also included are some questions and a brief summary of important points from each section. Keep in mind that the intention of this book is to challenge thinking and to stimulate self-evaluation. The most important revelations gained from this study may be something completely different from what the author intended. That's good. This book succeeds where it creates questions that lead to new insights; it fails where it claims to offer definitive answers. As the leader of your group, try to continually ask why people feel and think the way they do. This helps each individual be a good steward of the choices and decisions he or she makes.

Time

FOR STARTERS

To get the group thinking about the things that occupy our time, play this ice-breaker game called Speedball. Tell the group to line up (according to height, birthdate, alphabetical order of first name, last name, shoe size, amount of money in their pocket, etc.) for each category of question. They are to do this as quickly as they can. Then, call out: "favorite _____ (*book, movie, song, food, game, sport, place to shop, subject in school, etc.*)" and have each one answer in order as fast as she or he can. Don't give them time to think. If someone has no answer, pass that person. As soon as everyone has answered, reshuffle the group and call out a second "favorite _____." It should take no more than five to seven minutes to play four or five rounds of Speedball.

This is a good jumping-off point to talk about the ways we like to spend our time.

Video Suggestions

Movies, television, and literature have all held a fascination with the idea of time travel. Sometimes the movement is forward into the future; at other times it is back into the past. Always, there are terrible consequences when we tamper with time. Show a clip from a movie, such as one of the *Back to the Future* trilogy or *Time after Time*, or from a TV show such as *Quantum Leap*, and reflect on the following questions:

1. Why are people fascinated with the past? With the future?
2. If you could travel back in time, what would you like to change about yourself? About history? Why are these things important to you?
3. If you could travel into the future, what would you like to find out about yourself? Why?
4. What would you like to find out about the world? Why?
5. Since you can't travel through time, but are forever living in the present, how can you benefit from the past and work to create a good future?

Music Suggestions

The American Music Academy reported that, in the 1980s, the theme of *time* was the third most popular topic in music behind *relationships* (#1) and *violence* (#2). *World problems* and the *environment* ranked #4 and #5. Think of songs that deal with the issue of time. They can be found in pop, rock, heavy metal, rap, jazz, gospel—just about any genre of music. During the '80s, sixty-four different songs used the line, "time keeps slipping away" (or one very similar to it).

Why do people want to hold onto time?

Why do people think so much about getting older?

Try to find some songs that deal with time, and figure out what the artist is trying to say. What is the problem or issue, and how does the song resolve it? What is the mood of the song (happy, sad, angry, etc.)?

FOR PERSONAL REFLECTION

Think of all the things we do that "kill time" (television, video games, hanging at the mall/on the street, etc.). What's good about them? What's bad about them? Why do we like/dislike them?

Stewardship involves management. Do we manage "time killers," or do they manage us?

KEY POINTS

◇ Time is a gift from God.

◇ Time not managed is time wasted.

◇ We cannot change the past, but we can shape our future.

◇ We can't do everything, so we need to prioritize our uses of time.

◇ We should value other people's time as much as our own.

◇ The stewardship of time affects all areas of our life.

◇ We grow in Christian discipleship as we learn to appreciate and to manage our time.

Relationships

FOR STARTERS

Have the group sit in a large circle, and ask them to go quickly around the circle, telling their middle name, their favorite food, their mother's or father's name, their favorite subject in school, and the best birthday present they ever received. Next, have the entire group break into pairs, sitting back to back. Give each person a piece of paper, and have them write down the following information about the person behind them: eye color, what they are wearing, favorite food, favorite birthday present, and middle name. Call for a shift and have everyone pair with someone new. Ask them what kind of shoes the other person is wearing, whether the person is wearing a watch, what their favorite subject in school is, what their father's and/or mother's name is, and who they were just paired with a few minutes before. This exercise illustrates how important it is to pay attention to other people. Listening is a valuable skill for stewardship: listening to others and listening to God. (The true meaning of the word *obedience* is to attend to or to listen to.) No relationship can be sustained unless the participants pay attention to one another and develop good communication skills. This opens the topic of what qualities are important in making a relationship work.

VIDEO SUGGESTIONS

There are hundreds of movies made each year about relationships. We really want to get a handle on what makes a relationship work, why love feels the way it does, how to deal with losing loved ones, as well as how to find new people to love. Movies about relationships can help us realize that we're not the only ones who have ever had the feelings and experiences we have had. Take time to watch one of these "relationship" movies, or select clips from a variety of movies and reflect on the following questions:

1. How do the relationships develop in the film?

2. What do the characters get out of their relationships? What do they give to the other person? Why is the relationship important to them?

3. What do the characters learn about themselves in their relationships?

4. How are the characters changed by their relationships?

5. What lessons can be learned from the relationship(s) in the story?

MUSIC SUGGESTIONS

There is no end to the music about love, friendship, family, community, and society relationships. Get a copy of *Billboard Magazine's* top 100 singles in America. Make copies for everyone in the group. Have everyone mark the songs they know that have to do with relationships. As a group, listen to a sample of the songs and talk about why relationships make such good song material. Talk about group members' favorite songs dealing with relationships. Why do songs mean so much to us when we're in love? Deal with the emotions that songs are capable of making us feel. Music is a powerful teacher, and many of our attitudes about love come to us from the songs we hear.

PRAYER PARTNERING

Get a few new $1 bills from a local bank. Cut them in half and take them to a printshop to be laminated into wallet-sized cards. Shuffle the cards and distribute them to the group. Take a moment for everyone to find the other half of their dollar bill by matching serial numbers. People with matching pairs become prayer partners. Whenever the partners open their wallets or purses, they will be reminded to pray for their "other half."

Prayer is one of the most overlooked elements of relationships. We think of praying *to God*, but sometimes we forget to pray *for others*. It really builds a relationship to pray for someone else—and to know that the other person prays for you. It is almost impossible not to care about someone you are holding in your prayers. Another benefit of using the dollar bill is that it is a symbolic reminder that people are more important than money. It helps keep things in perspective.

FOR FURTHER DISCUSSION

An important topic of discussion for older youth, and particularly in retreat settings, is that of sexual relationships—a topic that is often on the minds of young men and women. The relationship between love and sex is quite complex, and the topic should not be avoided. Following are a dilemma, two biblical passages, and a group covenant that deal with the issue of our sexual stewardship.

Dilemma

Toni didn't know what to do. Her relationship with Chris had moved along so quickly that she wasn't sure of her true feelings. She loved Chris more than anyone she had ever known, but every time they were alone, Chris put moves on her to try to get her in bed. He kept telling her that if she loved him it would be okay. He also made her feel guilty by telling her that she must not care much about him if she didn't want to sleep with him. Part of her did want to have sex with him very badly, but another part of her was scared and doubtful. Toni wanted sex to be something special between herself and one other person. If Chris dumped her later, she would feel so used. Chris didn't seem to understand why she was reluctant. He kept pressuring her to make up her mind, and she just wasn't ready. She knew that, if it meant losing Chris, she would probably go to bed with him, but she didn't want it to be that way. Her friends told her to "go for it," but that just made it seem that much more wrong. Why did sex have to enter into love? It was so confusing.

1. What makes deciding to have sex with someone you love such a difficult decision?

2. In what ways is sex important to a love relationship? In what ways can sex actually harm a growing love relationship? If sex becomes too important in a relationship, what happens to communication and friendship?

3. How would you characterize the love Toni feels for Chris? The love Chris feels for Toni? What elements of a truly loving relationship do you feel are missing from their relationship?

4. In the list on the following page, which elements belong in a love relationship and which do not? Which elements might belong to both categories?

pressure	manipulation	patience
sexual relations	talking	listening
kissing	petting	ultimatums
giving gifts	respect	forgiveness
tolerance	time together	proving your love

Biblical Reflection

1 Corinthians 3:16-17; 6:12-20   Genesis 2:18; 21-25

1. It is obvious that God puts a high value on how we conduct ourselves as Christians. Why do you think marriage is seen as a prerequisite to sexual relations? What other kinds of commitment are as meaningful as a love commitment? How is making love in a sexual sense a commitment?

2. How does it change your feelings about sex to regard your body as a temple? How does it change your attitudes as you understand that your partner's body is a temple? How is the way we treat our love partner a reflection of our faith in God?

3. Respond to the statement: "Your sexuality is a gift from God." What does that mean to you? Do you agree or disagree?

4. If sexuality is a gift, then we have a responsibility to be good stewards of that gift. What does it mean to be a steward of sexuality? What is your responsibility to God? To your partner?

All the qualities of faithful stewardship—humility, appreciation, respect, accountability, the desire to serve, the ability to manage, etc.—are the same important qualities needed to make a strong, lasting love relationship. The sexual element of love is powerful and wonderful. There is nothing wrong or dirty about sex, but poor stewardship of the gift is a sin. Grasping the importance of faith in Christ in our love relationships helps to ensure that sex is kept in perspective and that it is a true expression of love that builds up the relationship, instead of a burden that can tear the relationship apart.

GROUP COVENANT

Often it is easier to stick to our conviction when we make a promise not only to ourselves and God, but to another person as well. Take time with your group to draft a STEWARDSHIP OF LOVE covenant in which you state, in your own words, your commitment to honor the body as a temple, to hold your sexuality as a sacred trust from God, and to make lasting commitments in their right and proper place. Sign your name to the covenant and have a copy made that you can keep. The key to loving another person totally is to first love yourself enough to know what you really want in a relationship. Such a covenant allows you to put into words what you truly believe in your heart.

KEY POINTS

◇ Our relationships are gifts to us from God.
◇ Strong relationships require management.
◇ We are stewards of other people's dignity, feelings, and respect.
◇ Stewardship requires that we care as much for the wants and needs of others as we care about our own wants and needs.
◇ The way we treat other people is the way we treat Jesus.
◇ Respect is a key element of the stewardship of relationships.
◇ Selfishness, partiality, prejudice, and apathy kill relationships.
◇ We feel better about ourselves as we become good stewards of all of our relationships.

Money and Possessions

FOR STARTERS

Play a game of popcorn. Have the group sit in a circle. Read a list of items and instruct everyone who has one of the items in their home to jump up and then sit right down. Read the list quickly. It should consist of items such as:

television	cordless telephone	microwave oven	computer
Nintendo	CD player	electric can opener	Walkman
VCR	calculator	dishwasher	vacuum cleaner
hairdryer	toaster oven	boom box	answering machine

Most of these things have become common in just the last thirty years. A few of them are only a decade old. Not long ago these were signs of privilege, but the 1990 census reported that 45 percent of all homes beneath the poverty level had a color television with cable TV, a microwave oven, at least two telephones, a stereo system, and in 12 percent of the homes there was also a personal computer.

How would our lives be different if these things did not yet exist? In what ways would our lives change? What would we do with the extra time and money available to us if we didn't have these things to spend them on?

Ask the members of the group to think of their favorite possession in the world. How did they get it? Did they buy it, or was it given to them? What makes it so special? What would it take for them to give it up?

VIDEO SUGGESTIONS

An excellent film for older groups is *Roger and Me*, the story of economic hard times in Flint, Michigan, that raises questions about wealth, power, the smashing of the American dream, and the responsibility we have to care for and about one another. Funny at times, horrifying at others, this movie strikes at the heart of the power of money and possessions in our lives.

A survey of TV commercials can reveal a lot about American values and our views concerning possessions. Ask critical questions about the ads. What are they saying about people who don't buy their product? What do they promise their product will do for you? What kinds of people are featured in their ads? What emphasis do they place on good looks, expensive clothes, position? What kinds of things are made to appear necessary for the good life?

How do these images shape our thinking? How many of the products being sold are necessary items? How many are luxury items? Why is it important for advertisers to make luxury items appear to be necessary items? What does that do to our value systems?

Look through a *TV Guide* magazine. Divide it into sections and have a race to see who can find the most programs dealing with money or possessions.

MUSIC SUGGESTIONS

Check out current songs and the people who sing them. What kind of lifestyle do the top ten singers/bands in America live? How do they model the "good life"? Do they seem to care about the consumers who buy their music, or do they care more about the money they make?

This extends not only to musicians but also to actors, professional athletes, writers, and other popular figures. Do most public figures in our world openly display good stewardship of their money, time, and talents? Can you think of examples of people in powerful positions who are good stewards? What makes them good stewards? Why do you think good stewards aren't necessarily more highly regarded than bad stewards?

Do singers and bands have a responsibility to promote strong values and provide good role models for the people who buy their music? Why or why not?

FOR PERSONAL REFLECTION

Find a copy of *Money* magazine, *Fortune*, *Forbes*, the *Wall Street Journal*, or another popular financial magazine or newspaper. Scan the articles and ads. What messages do you get from the publication? Do these publications display any concern for stewardship? How?

Would you say these magazines/newspapers imply that money is . . . The most important thing? Very important? Important? Necessary but not important? Unimportant?

Do magazines like these have any responsibility to teach that there are more important things in life than money and possessions? Why or why not?

KEY POINTS

◇ Money and possessions are gifts from God.
◇ Everything in creation really belongs to God; we merely use it.
◇ Money is a tool, not a goal.
◇ Charity is a sign of good stewardship.
◇ "Stuff" is good, but it won't make us happy or fulfilled.

◇ Money gives us the opportunity to serve God and neighbor.
◇ We should possess things, but not let things possess us.
◇ Stewardship does not mean doing *without*; it means doing *with integrity*.
◇ Money is temporary, but God's love is eternal.
◇ No one can serve two masters; no one can love both God and money.

Creation

FOR STARTERS

As people arrive, tape the name of an endangered species on their back without letting them see what it is. Instruct them to pantomime animal motions and make animal sounds as they travel through the room. Other people can read the name on their back and either nod or shake their heads if the person is making the wrong motion or sound. (Example: If someone with *African Elephant* is flapping his or her arms, people would shake their heads; walking on all fours would get a nod. Mooing would get a head shake; trumpeting would receive a nod.) When the participants think they know what species they are, they can make a guess. Allow about ten minutes for everyone to make guesses. Take a few minutes to talk about the plight of endangered species, including humankind.

VIDEO SUGGESTIONS

There are some great movies that deal with a variety of creation stewardship issues: environmental awareness and global politics (particularly in the science fiction genre), peace and justice issues, and others. *Gandhi* (over three hours long) and *Romero* are two examples of the many excellent films available for rental on such topics. Both films require some concentration and might lose younger viewers quickly. On television, programs such as *Network Earth* (TBS, CNN) and *National Geographic Explorer,* as well as a number of PBS and Discovery Channel programs deal with environmental issues in detail.

Music Suggestions

Get a copy of "Tame Yourself" (on Rhino tapes and CDs). ("Tame Yourself" is a collection of songs by various artists that was produced in 1991 for the benefit of PETA, "People for the Ethical Treatment of Animals.") You can develop a whole evening around the lyrics of the wide variety of songs in this collection. Don't ignore the work of Peter Gabriel, Sting, R.E.M., Bruce Cockburn, Elvis Costello, Joe Jackson, Midnight Oil, and the Fixx. Environmental issues have begun to appear in rap and country music as well. Performers are waking up to the problems of the planet. The music speaks powerfully to the plight.

Project Suggestions

Do a critical survey of your church and its environmental stewardship. Is it well maintained? Does it recycle? Does it use a lot of plastics and Styrofoam? Does it waste office supplies and copier papers? Is the plumbing in good shape? Does the furnace operate efficiently? Set up a recycling center. Make posters, collages, and bulletin boards that speak to environmental issues. Put a creation stewardship article in the church newsletter. Hold a stewardship education dinner. Prepare an environmental celebration for morning worship. Develop an environmental missions fund.

Letter writing is one of the most effective ways to change behavior. Two books in particular provide excellent suggestions on ways we can be involved in environmental stewardship issues: *You Can Make a Difference*, by Richard Zimmerman and *The Environmental Almanac*, compiled by World Resources Institute. Both volumes provide guidelines for writing letters and include information on persons/organizations to whom you can write to express your concern. A listing of pro-environmental groups is included, as well as the names of the most serious offenders.

The Earthworks Group publishes a very successful series of *50 Things You Can Do . . .* booklets that deal with a variety of stewardship issues. *Global Economics* by Ian McCrae is a great book for exploring the more socio-political/economic stewardship issues.

There are a number of great environmental magazines: *Garbage, E, World Watch, Buzzworm*, and *Earthwatch* are among the very best.

The World Wildlife Federation, Greenpeace, World Watch Institute, Sierra Club, and Audubon Society all list a wide variety of resources available for use in presentations. Most are very friendly and helpful when working with church groups.

The most exciting way to be a steward of creation is to get involved with a group that is making a difference. To be a part of a healing ministry is both fun and rewarding. Our own General Board of Global Ministries, through their World Program Division, Women's Program Division, Mission Education Division, and the UMCOR information hotline, can provide plenty of information concerning The United Methodist Church's involvement in addressing these important issues.

KEY POINTS

◇ Everything was created by God and is a gift to us.
◇ We are not the owners, but the caretakers.
◇ We should strive to return the earth to God in better shape than we received it.
◇ Creation stewardship does not include just plants, animals, and the planet; it includes everyone living on earth as well.
◇ Creation stewardship forces us to look ahead to the next generation.
◇ Education and involvement are the best weapons against global destruction.
◇ Dominion means we have power and authority, but it does not mean we can act without wisdom.
◇ We represent the Lord as stewards; therefore, our actions and practices reflect on God.

A WORSHIP OPTION

Prepare a place for worship. Place a table in the center of a circle of chairs, and upon the table place a candle, a watch, a ring, a coin, and a branch. These are symbols of time, relationships, money and possessions, and creation under the light of Christ. Have index cards, a pen, and a basket on the table. The hymn numbers cited in the following service are from *The United Methodist Hymnal.*

Gather together in a circle so that everyone can see everyone else. Assign readers or ask for volunteers for the scripture reading. Have hymnals or song sheets available for each member of the group.

A Stewardship Covenant Service

A LITANY PRAYER

Leader: In the beginning, God created. God created the heavens and the earth. God created the waters and the land. God created the greater and lesser lights. God created the animals of the land, the birds of the air, and the fish of the sea. God created the mountains and the forests. God created a man and a woman. God leaned back from creation with satisfaction and rested. God looked at all that had come into being. It was good.

Group: Creator God, thank you for the beauty of your earth, for the wonder of nature, for the miracle of life. Teach us to have eyes that see this world as you see it. Help us to appreciate all that you have done. Help us to manage it wisely, that in time we may hope to hear, "Well done, my good and faithful steward."

Leader: The Lord saw that Adam was alone and that it was not good, so God caused a sleep to fall upon Adam, and God created another person to be companion and helper, soulmate, and partner. God has always intended us to be gifts to one another. Separately we are incomplete; together we find wholeness.

Group: **Thank you, O Lord, for the gift of other people, for family and friends, for partners and soulmates, for helpers and companions, for the opportunity to share life with others. Teach us to value this most awesome gift and to be the very best people we can be for others. Help us appreciate the Christ in others, and enable us to be good stewards, that the Christ in us might be seen by others.**

Leader: The Lord looked upon the people and saw that they were a restless lot. Never satisfied with what they had, Adam and Eve set the stage for all future generations. Faced with the choice of living in the protective garden or setting out to make their own way, Adam and Eve chose the latter. By God's goodness, human beings were created with a great capacity for invention and advancement. Even God was impressed by the ingenuity and conviction with which humans set to the task of building the Tower of Babel. God placed every resource at the disposal of humankind, gave them boundless creativity and vision, and offered them the freedom to reach for the stars.

Group: **Thank you, O Lord, for the good gifts of this life: for the many fun and enjoyable things, for the things that make our lives easier, safer, healthier, and more meaningful. Help us to not take for granted these many good gifts, but teach us to use them wisely, not only for our own benefit, but also for the benefit of our neighbors. Fill our hearts with the desire to share generously, in gratitude for all that we have first received. Never allow us to make false gods of our possessions, but make us faithful to you in all ways, through Jesus Christ. Amen.**

A Hymn of Praise and Thanksgiving
"Now Thank We All Our God," No. 102

A Joyful Response
Psalm 150

A Reading from the Epistles
1 Corinthians 4:1-2

A Hymn of Celebration
"Unto Us Is Given" to the tune of *Holy, Holy, Holy!*

UNTO US IS GIVEN

Unto us is given, many gifts and blessings,
    Many ways to serve our Lord, with heart and soul and voice
Unto us is given, hope for all creation
    Let all God's people give thanks and rejoice

Unto us is given, the gift of the gospel
    Spread the news in all the world that Christ is Lord and King
God has freely given, mercy and salvation
    Praise God forever, lift your voice and sing.

Unto us is given, the gift of our neighbor
    Those we walk with day by day and those we never see
We are one communion, there is no distinction
    Made one in Christ for all eternity.

Unto us is given, the gift of creation
    All the glory of the earth God gives us to enjoy
Placed into our keeping, under our dominion,
    This sacred trust we must not dare destroy.

Unto us is given, many gifts and blessings,
    Many ways to serve our Lord, with heart and soul and voice
Unto us is given, hope for all creation
    Let all God's people give thanks and rejoice

WORDS: © 1993 by Dan R. Dick
MUSIC: John B. Dykes, 1861

A Reading from the Gospels
John 13:12-17

A Hymn of Commitment
"What Gift Can We Bring?", No. 87

A Time of Commitment to Faithful Stewardship
(All are invited to come to the table to write one or more ways in which they promise to improve their stewardship. The cards will be offered, consecrated, then displayed so that others may see the commitments made to God and the group.)

The Prayer of Consecration and Thanksgiving *(in unison)*
God of new beginnings, forgive what we have not been in the past, and help us to see what we can be for the future. Write the commitments we have made upon our hearts, that we might be new people, ready to assume the mantle of steward-ship, determined to grow in our faithfulness, prepared to prove our discipleship. Break the hardness of our hearts, and use us to do your healing, creating work. Bless the offerings and com-mitments we now make, to your honor and glory. We pray in the name of your Son, Jesus Christ our Lord. Amen.

A Reading from the Old Testament
Isaiah 6:1-8

A Hymn of Response
"Here I Am, Lord"

Benediction *(in unison)*
Each new day is a gift from God. Each person we meet holds for us a blessing. Each coin we receive has the power to serve. Each gentle brush of wind reminds us that the Spirit of Love and Life is with us. We go forth as God's stewards—chosen and beloved. Amen.

The Sharing of the Peace and Love of Christ